JOURNEY TO THE HEART

JOURNEY TO THE HEART

365-Day Guide to Thriving after Trauma

Svava Brooks

Educate4Change
Portland, OR
http://www.educate4change.com

Journey to the Heart
365-Day Guide to Thriving after Trauma

Copyright © 2016 by Svava Brooks

All rights reserved. This book is copyrighted and protected by law. No part of this book may be adapted, reproduced, stored, transmitted, or copied in any form without written permission from the publisher, except in the case of brief quotations used in critical articles and reviews.

ISBN-13: 9781539332862

ISBN-10: 1539332861

Cover design by Tracey Hale McIntyre

Dedication

I dedicate this book to my family: my husband, David, and my 3 children, Elisa, Sabrina, and David. I am eternally grateful for your love and support.

To my editor, Laura Stamps, for this divine partnership, and your encouragement to get my writing out to more people.

To all the survivors on the path to thriving, may this book help you reconnect with your truth.

Introduction

This book was written as a daily guide for the survivors of abuse or trauma. Each day features a little bit of "truth" to inspire you to think about a certain aspect of your healing journey.

Keep this book by your bedside. Read one section every morning for 365 days. Consider how the truth for that day applies to your past, present, and the trauma you survived.

As you allow each section to sink deeply into your heart and soul, you'll be taking another step forward on your healing journey. It doesn't matter whether you're at the beginning, middle, or in the last phase of your healing. If you work through this book day by day, you'll be making measurable progress.

After 365 days, you won't be the same person you used to be. You'll no longer be a Survivor. You'll be a Thriver. You'll finally be free. Free from the trauma of your past. Free of limitations. Free to create the life you desire.

How exciting!

Enjoy and much love to you,
Svava

Day #1

Today, create a vision of your healed life. On paper, list what your life would look like if you dropped your past, how amazing it would be, what your health would be like, where you would live, what kind of career success you'd have, and how happy you would be. Then feel all of this deep in your heart and soul. Every day invest more emotional energy into this happy vision than in your painful memories. Each time you do this, you're taking an important step toward healing.

Day #2

Survivors of child abuse and trauma often struggle with a variety of illnesses caused by chronic stress (trauma), like eating disorders, autoimmune diseases, allergies, thyroid conditions, intestinal issues, and many others. How is your health? If trauma has made you physically ill, it's more important than ever for you to remain on your healing journey. Healing from the mental and emotional effects of trauma often leads to healing from physical ailments.

Day #3

Support is vital on the healing journey. But have you ever thought about your spiritual support system? We can connect with God, our spiritual Source of support, whenever we feel overwhelmed and alone. Anytime. Any place. Wow! Are we lucky people, or what?

Day #4

Most of your pain comes from not accepting yourself. Self-acceptance is a vital skill you must learn. That will happen when you realize there's nothing wrong with you. And there never was.

Day #5

How do you reach out and ask for support when you don't know what you need? Admit this is a new skill for you. It's going to take practice. Give yourself permission to go slowly (baby steps). Be compassionate with yourself during this process. What baby step can you take today that will give you the confidence to reach out and ask for support?

Day #6

Maybe you were hurt by someone you loved and trusted. Maybe you were hurt by someone who claimed to love you. If that sounds familiar, it's easy to become confused about love and how normal loving behavior is supposed to look and feel. How do you fix that? Easy. Love feels good. Love never hurts.

Day #7

Scientists have recently discovered the stress from abuse or trauma affects our physical health in terrifying ways if it remains trapped in the body. Today, find a practice that will help you release trapped trauma like tapping, TRE, meditation, mindfulness, etc. Your body and your health will thank you!

Day #8

"Challenging" is a form of emotional abuse. This is someone who says "No" to everything you say or argues with everything you say, even simple things like the color of the sky. Does this sound like someone in your life right now? If so, now you know why this kind of behavior bothers you.

Day #9

Speak more of your truth every day, until you're comfortable with being more visible. In the process, you'll learn how to listen to others and allow them to be who they are in a relationship.

Day #10

Healing can be messy. No matter how bad it gets or how dark it feels, you can always find something to be grateful for. Hey, you're still alive, right? You can still take one breath after another. That's something. It may be all you have to be grateful for today, but it's enough.

Day #11

It takes time, but whenever you tell someone your story about the abuse or trauma you survived, you'll feel a little freer. Remind yourself every day of all the ways in which you're free now. This is one of those ways. Like love, personal freedom is an active process.

Day #12

Learning how to love is the key to your healing. Do something loving for yourself today. You deserve it!

Day #13

Diet is extremely important for healing the mind, body, and spirit. As a family, we have been shifting our diet to a more plant-based one, eating less meat and dairy and more fruit, leafy greens, and vegetables. It's been a challenging journey, but we feel good about the progress we've made. How about you? Have you considered making healthier choices in your diet?

Day #14

When you discover you've been talking to yourself in the same abusive way in which you had been treated as a child, it's like opening the door to a cage you've been imprisoned in your entire life. It's exhilarating to realize you can finally break free from this horrible inner critic, isn't it?

Day #15

We're all searching for connection. But too many times we think the connection we crave is external (outside ourselves, like people or stuff). It isn't. It's internal.

Day #16

Remember, there's nothing wrong with you. There never was, and there never will be. You're just like me, and there's nothing wrong with me. All you need is support, hope, and encouragement to find your way back home to yourself. And that's the truth!

Day #17

Begin today to live an authentic life of love and compassion. We're all connected. What we do to ourselves we do to others. Begin living an authentic life by sending prayers of love to everyone who crosses your path. Send these prayers to strangers, as well as people you know. It'll change your life and accelerate your healing.

Day #18

It's important to not only love yourself but also others. However, love and trust go hand in hand for abuse survivors. Trust is all about recognizing and paying attention to your inner warning system: red flags. Is your warning system "activated"? Do you see red flags when they pop up?

Day #19

I always practice mindfulness when I walk. It's a wonderful experience to be completely present for every step down the road. My heart expands with love in each moment, as I fully experience the beauty of this world. Have you ever practiced "walking mindfulness"? If not, try it today. The insight you gain will blow you away. Seriously!

Day #20

Part of healing is learning how to express your feelings. It's a new experience for abuse survivors and no bed of roses. Yeah, it's tough. All those bottled up emotions come pouring out: the good, the bad, and the really ugly. This can be an intense time for you and your partner. Be gentle with yourself. It'll get better.

Day #21

The abuse you survived wasn't your fault. It's not your fault now, and it never will be your fault. That's a fact.

Day #22

Old toxic beliefs are what prevent you from making big changes in your life. Don't give up on yourself. You can tackle any change, big or small, one slow step at a time. It just takes a plan, self-compassion, consistent effort, and support. What healthy change would you like to make in your life today?

Day #23

You can only be your authentic self when you listen to and follow your heart. No exceptions. But how do you do that if you're used to disconnecting from your heart and ignoring your intuition? Every time you need to make a decision, check with your heart first. Ask your heart if it feels this is the right decision for YOU? Is it the choice that will reap the most favorable outcome for YOU? Is it what YOU truly want? This is authenticity.

Day #24

Mindfulness (focusing on the present moment) helps you stay connected to yourself and everything in life. It forces you to focus on what you're doing in the present moment and prevents subconscious distractions, like worrying about the past or the future.

Day #25

The people in your life who feel threatened by the progress you're making on your healing journey are in your life because they subconsciously remind you of emotional abusers from your past. The wounded soul inside you attracted these people into your life. It wanted them to love and understand you. It wanted them to make it all better. This never works, as you know.

Day #26

One of the hardest parts of the healing journey is forgiving yourself for all the things you did before you began to heal. Have you forgiven yourself for the past? If not, make today the day you do that.

Day #27

It's important to see the perfection in our imperfections. Doing this will eventually end the toxic habit of being our own worst critic, which only sabotages your life.

Day #28

How can you help your brain change its default setting from "Survival Mode" to "Healing Mode"? Put a strong support system in place. You'll need support when you encounter resistance from your brain with each step you take on your healing journey. The brain is not fond of change.

Day #29

Here are two affirmations I said to myself years ago: ***1.) I am willing. 2.) I am willing to consider the possibility that I can heal.*** I still use them when my mind tells me I can't do something. Think about that today. Are you willing?

Day #30

When child abuse survivors grow up they find a tiny, safe space. Unfortunately, it's a trap. Are you stuck in the small, restricted world you've built for yourself? Take a careful look at every aspect of your life today. Healing requires risk. Are you trapped in certain areas of your safe world?

Day #31

When you only focus on the past or the future, you keep yourself off balance. Instead, focus on the present moment, the NOW. That's where you live. You do this by being grateful for what you already have. After all, the NOW is where you create the past and the future. Every morning and evening list all the things you have accomplished on your healing journey and express gratitude for each one. Enjoy your success in the NOW!

Day #32

Healing began for me on the day I realized there was a "civil war" going on inside me. Part of me (fear) demanded to be rescued. It lived in a fantasy world and truly believed someone would appear out of nowhere to save me. This toxic belief was holding me hostage. Do you want to be rescued too? It'll never happen.

Day #33

It's not about how many falls I've had (and will continue to have). It's about how I always find a way to get back up and move forward again. Don't forget this the next time you face a healing challenge. Just get back up. Remember to be kind to yourself. Keep moving forward. That's how you succeed on the healing journey.

Day #34

Surround yourself with positive, nourishing people for support. Never try to go it alone. Don't forget to tap into your "spiritual" support system. Meditate, journal, and pray every day. Whatever you need, God will always find a way to send it to you in the form of a teacher, coach, book, or helpful friend. That's a given!

Day #35

What is the healing journey all about? It's about reconnecting with who you truly are, which is your authentic self. What steps are you taking today to rediscover and reconnect with the real you?

Day #36

Child sexual abuse isn't about sex. It's about power. You had to give up your power in order to survive the abuse. But now you're an adult. Take back your power today!

Day #37

Believe me, when I was ready to heal from child abuse years ago I wasn't happy when I discovered this isn't a quick-fix process. In fact, I shed many tears over that fact. I had suffered for decades from the trauma of abuse. I was out of patience. I wanted to be perfectly healed, and I wanted it NOW! Are you feeling impatient about a certain aspect of your healing journey? If so, relax. All big changes take time. Healing from abuse and trauma are no different.

Day #38

Your body has much wisdom to teach you. Work with it rather than against it. It's amazing what you'll discover when you honor your body and listen to its message.

Day #39

If you're feeling desperate today, hand that burden over to God and ask for help. That's all you have to do. And it's a good thing because sometimes that's all you can do. Life is just too hard on those days to do anything else.

Day #40

Here's the truth about acceptance. No one can accept you but YOU. Trying to be perfect is a losing situation, because perfectionism has nothing to do with acceptance. That's why it never works.

Day #41

Many child abuse and trauma survivors desperately need support, but they aren't asking for it. How is that possible? Easy. As a survivor, you don't know what you "need." Before you can ask for support, you must not only be aware of your feelings but also comfortable expressing them. Not an easy task for trauma survivors. The brain disconnects from the body during trauma. If you've been hesitating and don't know why, this is the reason.

Day #42

If you practice self-care, self-love, and self-compassion every day, you'll soon realize the power inside you isn't just an average power. It's a super power. And it's the real YOU!!

Day #43

Yes, you can heal. Yes, you can create a normal, healthy life for yourself. Begin by cherishing the awesome person you were before the abuse or trauma. That's your true identity.

Day #44

"Gaslighting" is a form of emotional abuse. This is when someone twists reality by denying his/her actions, hurtful words, promises, etc. The goal is to make you doubt your sanity. Does this sound like someone from your past or someone in your life today? Now you know why you always feel confused and anxious around this person. No, you're not crazy. This is a devastating form of emotional abuse.

Day #45

Practice becoming visible as an adult. No need to hide anymore. No one is going to harm you. You're an adult now. Keep practicing your truth, speaking up, setting personal boundaries, and standing firm on them. Eventually, you'll overcome your fear and stop waiting for the other shoe to drop every time you say something.

Day #46

The happier you are with yourself, the more content you'll be with your life. Why? You know you're loved. You've learned how to love yourself. You know how to love. And that makes you free. Life will still present challenges, but you'll know how to handle them, because you love and trust yourself.

Day #47

The trauma and abuse I survived as a child wasn't what hurt the most. It was the fact I didn't have anyone to tell about it. Does that sound like you? If so, that secret will hold you hostage until you're able to tell someone your story in a safe place with safe people, who validate and encourage you. Find that safe friend or support group today. You need to tell someone.

Day #48

Why do I always encourage you to place your hand on your heart? It activates Oxytocin, the body's "happiness" hormone. It's responsible for producing feelings of contentment, calmness, and serenity. Too cool, huh? And it works!

Day #49

As you move forward on your healing journey and learn how to listen to your heart, you'll find it needs different things from time to time. For example, I've always played hard, thriving on noise and lots of action. But now my heart craves more quiet time, like peaceful hikes in the woods, meditation, and yoga. So I'm honoring that. What is your heart asking for today? Whatever it needs, honor it.

Day #50

Don't try to love other people by your own effort. You can't. Instead, relax and allow the Love of God to flow through you to everyone you meet. That's how it works.

Day #51

You already have everything you need to heal and restore. You're an amazing reservoir of creativity and strength. Use that truth to claim your healing today!

Day #52

Do you know there's nothing wrong with you? It's true! How do I know? Because I'm just like you, and there's nothing wrong with me. Did you know most people think there's something wrong with them? It's part of the universal human condition. But the truth is there's nothing wrong with these people. And there's nothing wrong with you either. Think about that today.

Day #53

You are Love. You are Love in all you see. Send Love to all you see. Today, send Love freely with no attachment to how, when, or where it will manifest. That's true freedom.

Day #54

Why does the healing journey take so long? Good changes develop slowly over time. They occur in stages. It's important to experience and move through each stage. Be patient. You're doing just fine!

Day #55

Sweet friend, listen to me. I want you to allow this to sink deeply into your soul today. You are already perfect enough, loveable enough, and good enough. Do something good for yourself NOW. Don't wait. Don't attach a condition to it. Just do it. You're more than worth it.

Day #56

Marriage can be rough when you're healing from child abuse or trauma. Some days you want your partner to stay. Some days you want to be alone. It's important to ask for what you need, even during those times when all you can say is, *"Honey, I'm having a meltdown right now...I just need to cry...don't worry...you didn't do anything wrong...it's not your fault...just hold me if you can...tell me everything is going to be okay."*

Day #57

Notice how love manifests in your everyday life. The big ways and the small ways. If you practice this, subtle changes will ripple through your life. Soon that ripple will become a stream, then a river, then an ocean of Love. Submerge yourself in it. This is how Love works. It's limitless and available to us all the time.

Day #58

Our passion is our fuel. It's what keeps us going no matter how many challenges come our way. Our passion also protects us. As long as we're pursuing it, we don't care what other people think about it, or if we're doing it perfectly. Why? Because what we're passionate about gives us joy. What are you passionate about today?

Day #59

We exist in a world where we've been taught from the time we're tiny children to trust others more than ourselves. This kind of teaching is terribly damaging to the soul. Do something today to prove to your soul that you trust your inner wisdom and guidance.

Day #60

One way you can tell you're healing is by the sudden desire to reach out and help others in need. Some feel led to help other survivors of trauma or child abuse. Others reach out in different ways. Have you been thinking about this lately? If so, congratulations. You're healing!

Day #61

The people in your life who feel threatened by the progress you're making on your healing journey are those who were invested in your pain because they benefitted from it in some way. Don't let them get to you. Don't allow them to sabotage your healing. Keep moving forward, regardless of the hurtful things they might say or do to stop you.

Day #62

It's never too late to learn how to love yourself. You can't heal completely until you do. Best of all, the more you love yourself, the more love you'll feel toward others, and the more love you'll receive. Wow, right?!

Day #63

What do you do to ground yourself? I love to start my day in nature. Surrounded by the amazing trees in my yard, I feel supported, nurtured, and grounded in the natural realm. How about you? Ground yourself in the way that works best for you every morning. It'll keep you on track with your healing journey.

Day #64

Every time you take a step forward on your healing journey, your brain will freak. It's not fond of change. Your brain will sound the alarm and try to convince you things aren't that bad (yes, they are!), you don't need to heal (yes, you do!), and you're doing fine (no, you're not!). Don't listen to it. Don't allow your brain to hold you hostage with these old, toxic coping patterns.

Day #65

Develop the habit of following your heart every day. Try it right now. Allow your heart to lead your life. How? By asking your heart questions, especially if you're unsure about what to do in a certain situation. You'll be blessed with wonderful, heartfelt answers. When you follow your heart, you're honoring and valuing your authentic self.

Day #66

Trust is about relationships: a relationship with yourself, a relationship with the world, a relationship with other people, and a relationship with God. How do your relationships in these areas look today?

Day #67

Every Monday morning I start my week with focused intention. It makes all the difference. How do you do this? Start a journal and list 5 things you're grateful for. Then list 3 things you're doing this week that will help you manifest one of your goals. Show this list to a safe friend or your support group.

Day #68

Listen to your heart. It's trying to set you free from fear. Your heart is grounded in reality, not fantasy. It knows no one is coming to rescue you. If you listen to it, your heart will tell you that you don't need to be rescued. You already have everything inside you to heal and restore.

Day #69

Your individual challenges are an important part of your personal journey. Because of that, you should respond to them with kindness. Especially kindness to yourself. How do you plan to be kind to yourself today?

Day #70

For many years I avoided my negative emotions. They terrified me. I felt like they were so intense I would never understand them or express them safely. I was wrong. Now my negative emotions have become my friends. When I struggle with them, I know that's a sign I need to tweak some aspect of my life that no longer nourishes me.

Day #71

Accepting the abundance surrounding us is a skill we must learn for ourselves. Receiving is a vital part of that process. For example, when you accept a gift with gratitude, you're giving a positive gift back to the universe and to the person who gave you the gift. The same is true when you smile at people or say something kind and compassionate to everyone you meet. You're opening a space for more abundance. See how that works?

Day #72

Negative emotions are your GPS. Don't ignore them. Friend them and allow them to guide you toward the healthy, happy, nourishing life you've always wanted. That's their true purpose.

Day #73

Healing from trauma and abuse isn't a quick fix. It won't happen overnight or in just a few days, weeks, or months. That's not how it works. Change happens slowly, one small step at a time. Keep moving forward on your healing journey. You're on the right path.

Day #74

Every time you feel a negative emotion overwhelm you (anger, anxiety, grief, sadness, etc.), don't let it sweep you away. Instead, step back and play "detective." Watch and observe this feeling, until it tells you exactly what it is, what triggered it, and why. Then release it in a healthy way by allowing it to flow through your body and out. Soon you won't panic when these feelings appear out of nowhere. Instead, you'll learn to enjoy the investigative process. After all, it's setting you free.

Day #75

You know me. I'm a spiritual person. Every time I felt like I just couldn't take another step on my healing journey, I would fall to my knees and pray. God never let me down. Afterwards, I always felt better and could sense his support. That pulled me out of whatever emotional muck I was wading through at the time. He will do the same for you.

Day #76

We often feel the abuse or trauma we endured was our fault. We didn't do something right, because we weren't perfect enough. Of course, that's a lie. There wasn't anything we could have done. Yet we tried to be perfect so it won't happen again. But perfectionism is exhausting, and it never works. If you still have perfectionist tendencies, list all of them on a sheet of paper, and then find ways to be gloriously imperfect in every one of those areas. Being beautifully imperfect is such FUN. Try it today and see!!

Day #77

It's not unusual for child abuse and trauma survivors to feel alone, disconnected, and misunderstood. You think no one cares or wants to support you. True, there may not be any compassionate, supportive people in your life. But you may not be asking for support either. If that sounds like you, why aren't you reaching out for support?

Day #78

Explore the truth of who you are. What makes you happy? What brings you joy? What gives you peace? Make a list and do these things. Only when you do them for yourself will you reconnect with your inner personal power.

Day #79

If you have come to think the abuse or trauma you survived was your fault in some way, you'll spend the rest of your life trying to change, to become different, to be better, perfect. So far that hasn't worked for you, has it? Know why? Because there was never anything wrong with you. The abuse wasn't your fault. Period.

Day #80

How can you tell you're healing? You've freed yourself from the burden of shame, and you're comfortable sharing your story with others.

Day #81

When you spent your childhood perfecting the skill of staying silent and becoming invisible, how do you change that toxic pattern as an adult? You begin slowly by speaking up, one conversation, one thought, one opinion at a time. Do this with people you know are safe, like your peer support group.

Day #82

If you're struggling today, be gentle with yourself. Be kind to yourself. Put your hand on your heart to comfort yourself. Be there for yourself.

Day #83

How can you experience personal freedom? For me, it began when I told that first person about the abuse I had suffered as a child. Have you told that first person yet about the abuse or trauma you survived? Choose a safe friend, and tell that person today.

Day #84

Why should you place your hand over your heart? Because it validates your existence. It demonstrates in the physical realm that you're giving yourself the love and kindness you needed but never received as an abused child.

Day #85

May you be loved. May you feel peace. May you be blessed beyond measure. This is my wish for you today. But this won't happen until you accept yourself fully and know deep in your soul that you are loved by yourself and by God. It all starts with you.

Day #86

Today, take a few minutes to send divine Love energy out to the person standing next to you, to your neighborhood, your state, and your country. The world needs more lovers and peacemakers. The world needs you!

Day #87

Resistance to the present moment is a toxic coping skill. To discover what you're resisting, begin by creating a safe zone to manage your thoughts and beliefs. Then allow your subconscious to slowly bring to mind what it's been holding on to and resisting from your traumatic past. Now you're ready to face it and heal.

Day #88

Survivors of abuse, especially emotional abuse, are trapped by trauma. It's fueled by shame and fear. Trauma isolates, disconnects, and distorts. But you don't have to remain trapped. Because you're on a healing journey, every step along the way will help you blossom into the grounded, compassionate, trusting human being you were born to be. Don't give up. It will happen!

Day #89

Practice the art of receiving today. Receive, receive, receive. Make today a miracle-filled day!!

Day #90

Change is initially a mental exercise, so the first stage is governed by willpower and excitement. In the second stage, you create a routine to support this new change, which helps you deal with emotional resistance. By the time you progress to the third stage, this new change has become a lifestyle.

Day #91

Survivors are incredibly hard on themselves. It's the main way we prevent love from blessing us. We feel we're unlovable, or we don't deserve love. We attach conditions to love, like: *"When I am (blank) enough, I can have (whatever good thing I would like)."* This is a toxic lie. The truth is you're already good enough. Give yourself that good thing you want today.

Day #92

Boundaries define the difference between your responsibilities as an adult and other people's responsibilities as adults. Everyone is supposed to do their part. If someone crosses one of your boundaries or pressures you to cross a boundary, that's a "red flag."

Day #93

Loving others begins with the way you care for yourself. That's the first step. You learn to feel grateful for who you are. You become willing to explore the ways in which you struggle with loving and accepting yourself.

Day #94

Every day you should feed your mind with thirty minutes of information about empowerment, change, and healing from trauma. How do I do this? I work it into my busy day. I listen to an audiobook when I go for a run. I watch a short video when I take a work break. I read a few pages of a book before I fall asleep at night. When I'm waiting in line, I read an ebook on my cell phone. How can you work thirty minutes of healing information into your busy day?

Day #95

I tell everyone I love them, and I mean it. My kids, husband, friends, clients, you name it. We could all use more love. We need people who are willing to send love out into this world 24/7. It's a wonderful way to live! You can do this, too. Why not start today?

Day #96

Emotional abandonment is very painful. Abused children have to find a way to disconnect from the pain in order to survive it. What worked best for me was to stay distracted. I made sure I was so busy there wasn't time to think or feel. Distraction is a toxic coping skill. When I'm distracted, I'm disconnected. Does this sound like you?

Day #97

Healing will change the dynamic of all your relationships. There will be those who applaud the progress you're making on your healing journey. Others will feel threatened and attack. This is normal.

Day #98

How can you tell you're healing? You no longer have the need to be in control all the time.

Day #99

Focus your intent on the positive every morning. If you don't, you're subconsciously giving up control of your day. Instead, stay consciously in charge. Create the nourishing, empowered life you desire one day and one intention at a time.

Day #100

Your brain is hardwired to protect you. The part of the brain that takes over when you're scared is the part that wants to keep you safe (Survival Mode). In the case of chronic abuse and trauma, the safety response is the part of the brain we use the most. Unfortunately, "Survival Mode" is not "Healing Mode." Don't allow your brain to sabotage your progress. It just needs time to adjust. And you need a good support system in place to help you through this transitional period.

Day #101

Is self-care selfish? No, not at all. You can't truly love anyone in a healthy way unless you do the very best job you can loving yourself first. That's why self-care should be your top priority every day. Is self-care at the top of your list every day? If not, why?

Day #102

Trusting yourself leads to trusting God. Eventually, you begin to feel like everything is going to work out, even the aspects of your life you can't control. You get to the point where you trust yourself enough to let go of those things so you can trust in God's plan for your life.

Day #103

Your thoughts have creative power. You have the freedom to choose which thoughts to accept/believe and which thoughts to reject. Amazing, right? Choose wisely. Choose positive thoughts.

Day #104

Being stuck isn't fun. I know. I've been there. Break free today. Reach out for support!

Day #105

Living an authentic life is not about pretending you don't have challenges. It's not perfectionism. It's about accepting every challenge that comes your way as a part of being human.

Day #106

Support is the fast track to success! What kind of support system do you have in place today to help you reach your healing goals? Is it still strong, or do you need to add to it? Tweak it a little by adding a new support group or forum, signing up with a new coach, or reaching out to a friend.

Day #107

We live in an abundant universe. All you have to do is remain open to the abundance flowing toward you. How are you remaining open today to receive all the abundance flowing toward you?

Day #108

When a sudden sense of fear comes over you, don't run from it. Embrace it. Concentrate on it. When you do, it will tell you why it appeared. It's either trapped fear from the past or a red flag. Pay attention to it. Then you can decide what kind of action to take.

Day #109

Do you realize you already have all the power you need to heal? You do! You just need to learn how to find the path back to your heart, so you can become the awesome person you were destined to be. That's what the healing path is all about. Stay on it. You're doing GREAT!!

Day #110

Practicing mindfulness will help you dig deeper when you realize a layer of resistance has been triggered. For example, suddenly you'll notice you're feeling something, thinking something, responding to something. What is it?? Go after it like a detective until you solve this mystery.

Day #111

Healing can be messy. There were many times when I was down on my knees, lost and confused, pleading with God for a little light at the end of the tunnel. He never let me down. Are you in that place today? Send out a plea for help to your Higher Power. You won't be disappointed!

Day #112

If you're just beginning to reconnect with your body, emotions, and other people, the first place to start is with nature. Go outside and connect with the earth and sky. Practice pulling this powerful, loving, compassionate, spiritual energy into yourself.

Day #113

Why am I a fan of peer support groups? Because you learn so much in one, like how others are healing, what works and what doesn't work on the healing journey, and how it feels to be believed, validated, and heard. Have you joined a peer support group yet? If not, take a chance and do it today. You'll feel so much better. I guarantee it!

Day #114

You have the power to take care of yourself, to speak up when you need to protect a boundary, or to ask for help. Use it. This is how you create healthy relationships and attract good people into your life.

Day #115

Abuse and trauma victims often believe the pain they endured was their fault in some way. They begin to think there's something wrong with them that caused this horrible thing to happen. The truth is there's nothing wrong with you, and there never has been. Let that truth sink deeply into your soul today.

Day #116

Your truth defines your emotional boundaries. This is your truth: you are a precious spirit of Divine Love, who deserves to be treated with love and respect. No exceptions. Unfortunately, abusers have extremely low self-esteem and enjoy violating emotional boundaries. Don't allow them to violate yours. No exceptions!

Day #117

Most child abuse survivors spent their childhoods perfecting the skill of silence and becoming invisible. It was a great strategy for survival. Because of that, it's very hard for them to learn how to be visible as adults. It feels like rocking the boat. We're so used to abusers twisting everything we say to use it against us. It's terrifying for us to ask for what we need or to enforce personal boundaries when we weren't allowed to practice these vital human skills as children. Be gentle with yourself. You'll learn.

Day #118

Once you set emotional boundaries, you'll have to protect and defend them. That's a must. Do this by using the abuser's favorite word: NO. Calmly say, *"No, I don't agree with that,"* or *"No, that's not true about me,"* or *"No, that's not what I think."* Then walk away. Never argue with an abusive person. You can't win an insane argument.

Day #119

What does your body crave today? Listen carefully. Then give it the loving care it needs.

Day #120

Why should you get in the habit of supporting yourself by placing your hand over your heart? Because it allows your heart to feel warmth from the hand of someone you've learned to trust completely: YOU!

Day #121

It was shocking to discover how much I rejected love in the past. But it makes sense when you think about it. If you're a survivor of abuse, there were people in your past you loved, who hurt you deeply. You begin rejecting love to protect yourself from being hurt again. Are you rejecting love for this reason, too?

Day #122

How do you talk to yourself? Think about it. Do you talk to yourself in the same abusive manner in which you were treated as a child? Are you unkind, harsh, and super critical of yourself in every way?

Day #123

Much of surviving child abuse involves "resistance." After all, it helped you disconnect and survive the trauma of abuse. But this amazing childhood survival skill is toxic to your adult life. The stress from resisting both good and bad change will eventually destroy your health and wellbeing. Do you have a chronic illness that refuses to heal completely? Resistance could be the root cause.

Day #124

How do you break the power of fear? You talk to it like an old friend. Let it know you hear it and see it. Feel it rising up in your body. Tell it you appreciate its concern, but you're not a terrified child anymore. You're an adult. You can handle this. Then tell it to set itself free. Wave goodbye to it.

Day #125

We all know giving to others is important. But so is learning how to receive. Open yourself to receiving miracles today from any place, person, or thing.

Day #126

Good change only becomes a lifestyle after you confront and resolve each area of resistance you encounter along the way. You must look those fears in the eye, assure your inner child he/she is safe, and convince this child the new change is good. Only then can you make peace with the resistance and work through it.

Day #127

My advice to every abuse survivor? When you're ready, find your voice and tell your story. It matters. You matter. You'll be helping countless survivors find the courage to tell their stories. They'll look at you and realize they can heal and restore, too. You are a gift to many. Don't hide your Light. Let it shine!

Day #128

How can you reactivate your internal warning system? What can you do if you've ignored "red flags" for so long you don't notice them anymore? A good place to start is an abuse survivor group, where you can practice reactivating your internal system within the safety of a community you trust. You can also practice mindfulness. It will train you to pay more attention to what's happening around you.

Day #129

To love and to be loved isn't just a mental process. It's also an active process. You've got to walk your talk. Words without corresponding action are meaningless to yourself and to the people you love. How have you been actively demonstrating love this week to yourself and to others?

Day #130

You can successfully tackle any change if the action is repetitive. It has to become a habit before it can feel like a normal part of your life. Consistent effort during the first four weeks is the key.

Day #131

When you love, you love. Period. Here's a secret I've discovered about living a life of Love. When you love, more love comes into your life. You always attract the same energy you put forth. What kind of energy have you been putting forth this week? If it's not Love energy, change that.

Day #132

Distraction is a toxic coping skill. It's how we learn to deal with any kind of discomfort. Our subconscious immediately wants to dull the pain of any uncomfortable situation by distracting us. Don't allow your subconscious to get away with that any longer. When you feel the need to do too much, force yourself to slow down and shorten your To-Do List. Become aware of what's really happening here.

Day #133

If you're not depressed, anxious, lonely, grieving, frustrated, perfect, or taking care of someone else, who are you? Ever thought about that?

Day #134

How can you tell you're healing? You're able to listen to someone else's story of abuse or trauma, while holding a safe place for yourself.

Day #135

The healing journey is the path back to your heart, to self-acceptance, to self-love, to divine grace. This is the place where you connect with God. It's where you know deep in your heart you're incredibly valuable, and you always have been. This is your truth. Claim it today!

Day #136

How can you help your brain change its default setting from "Survival Mode" to "Healing Mode"? Gather as much information as you can about healing and the healing journey. You need to be well-prepared for resistance from your brain as you move forward with your healing. The brain is not fond of change.

Day #137

Love is a spiritual essence. It's what we are as spiritual beings. Once you receive this revelation of Love, make it your focus. When you begin to live it, life become easier, more peaceful, and enjoyable. It's an awesome way to live!

Day #138

Personal challenges teach us how to help ourselves, so we can pass that knowledge to others. Don't be afraid to offer what you've learned on your healing journey to someone in need. You'll be helping that person more than you realize.

Day #139

Start looking at life in a positive way. With every positive thought and word, you're training your brain to help you become the happy, healthy, successful person you've always dreamed of being. How? The chemical composition and physical structure of your brain is changed from surviving to thriving. This is important, because everything begins in the brain.

Day #140

All survivors of child abuse want to heal. We really do. But when given the chance, we rarely leap at it. Instead, we hesitate and hold back. In what area of your healing journey are you hesitating today?

Day #141

Who is the "real" you? We're all the same. We're Love and Light. Allow this truth to sink deeply into your heart and soul today.

Day #142

What kind of support have you put in place to help you manifest your goals? Maybe you think you don't need support. Maybe you think you can do this alone. I understand completely. I tried the same thing. It didn't work. I just kept spinning my wheels. Very frustrating! I didn't begin to manifest my healing goals until I joined a few support groups and surrounded myself with other child abuse survivors.

Day #143

The hardest thing for abuse and trauma survivors to do is to connect with other people. Yet, as human beings, we're all driven to connect. Reconnection begins with YOU. Learn how to value yourself. Learn how to love yourself. Take that first step today. It'll make a big difference in the success of your healing journey.

Day #144

Do you need to limit your exposure to negative coworkers, family, or friends? If so, think about doing that today.

Day #145

An abuse survivor's mind works in toxic ways. It wants to rationalize. It wants to convince you the abuse was your fault. It wants you to believe the trauma you experienced was an isolated incident. None of this is true. If you're struggling with these toxic thoughts, allow this truth to sink deeply into your heart and soul today: the abuse wasn't your fault. It wasn't an isolated incident. You're not alone.

Day #146

It's easy to focus on your mind when you're dealing with trauma. But the body is incredibly wise. The body knows what you need to experience in order to heal. It knows which layers of resistance you're ready to break through to discover the "real" you. Befriend your body, mind, and spirit. This is how you uncover toxic beliefs and resistance.

Day #147

I've always been a spiritual person. But, believe it or not, the process of healing from child abuse only deepened my faith. Early in my healing journey I discovered a connection with God just made the whole process easier. How has your faith helped you with your healing from abuse or trauma?

Day #148

If you've never practiced reconnecting by connecting with nature, the overwhelming support of this grounding energy will feel awesomely good! Or it can be terrifying. I understand. At the beginning of my healing journey I resisted anything I didn't understand, too. But the more I practiced this kind of reconnecting the more real it became. Try it today.

Day #149

What will you learn in a peer support group? You'll learn you're not alone, there's nothing wrong with you, and the abuse or trauma wasn't your fault. If you've been thinking about joining a peer support group, take a chance and do it today. You'll be glad you did!

Day #150

As you progress on your healing journey, you'll lose a few "friends" along the way. Don't worry. This is normal. Those who truly love and value you will stick with you. Those who only "liked" you because they could use you will leave. Good riddance, right?

Day #151

Sometimes you may wonder if you will ever heal from abuse or trauma. At times, the path to recovery feels like trying to put together a jigsaw puzzle with pieces missing. Believe it or not, the healing process isn't complicated. It's simple. But healing can be blocked by toxic beliefs. Are you struggling to fix yourself because you believe there's something wrong with you? If so, this toxic belief is blocking your healing. Jumpstart your healing today with this fact: there's nothing wrong with you, and there never has been.

Day #152

We all deserve to be treated with love and respect. This is one of your most important boundaries. Those who cross it don't value you. Make sure everyone in your inner circle of friends recognizes and values your worth.

Day #153

One terribly damaging form of emotional abuse is constantly interrupting, changing the subject, or negating everything a person says. This kind of abuse invalidates that person's existence and encourages the toxic strategy of silence.

Day #154

If you're learning how to defend your emotional boundaries, be patient with yourself. This isn't an easy task for survivors of child abuse. It can take up to six months to feel comfortable defending your emotional boundaries. But practice makes perfect. And it will get easier. I promise!

Day #155

Why do I always tell you to place your hand on your heart? Because it's a way of gently reminding yourself that you are loved, and you're here for yourself. If you've been resisting this practice, try it today. You'll see what I mean.

Day #156

Today, I'm listening to my body, and it tells me it needs yoga and stillness. So that's my top priority at the moment. I serve my clients best when I take gentle, compassionate care of myself. You're no different. You operate best when you make self-care a top priority, too. Put yourself at the top of your To-Do list. Not at the bottom.

Day #157

What are you rejecting? Do you reject love whenever it's offered to you? I did. I spent years hiding from love, because I didn't feel worthy of it. Now I welcome love each and every day. Accept any love that comes your way today. It feels great!

Day #158

The suffering and abuse you survived had nothing to do with God. So why didn't he rescue you? He did! He helped you survive the abuse. He's holding your hand right now every step of the way, as you heal from trauma and abuse. Even if you give up on yourself, God will never give up on you. Never.

Day #159

You're not the abusive or traumatic things that happened to you. You're so much more. The truth is you're a gift and a blessing. Embrace that today. Allow it to sink deeply into your soul, until you believe it, too.

Day #160

Fear is fueled by fear. The more fearful you become, the more power you give it. Don't allow this to happen. Because of your traumatic or abusive past, fear will always be a part of who you are. But don't give it control. Break its power the minute it appears.

Day #161

I start each morning with a positive intention to give the day a powerful boost in the right direction. Then I remain open to any miracles that come my way. Try this today and watch what happens!

Day #162

Is there a way to speed up the healing process? No. The fact the healing journey takes so long can be frustrating, I know. Especially when you're exhausted from struggling with the aftereffects of abuse. However, your need for "speed" is part of your coping pattern. It's a toxic coping skill. Who knew, right?

Day #163

At some point in your healing journey, you'll realize you have to make a choice. It's time to choose healing. No more playing at this. No more hiding from your abusive past. No more denying the secret shame of what happened to you in the past and how much it still hurts. It's time to tell your story to a safe person. Do that today. If you've already done that, find another safe person to tell today. Every time you do this you'll experience freedom from your past.

Day #164

When you notice a "red flag" pop up in a situation or conversation, are you still in the toxic habit of reasoning it away? You might tell yourself, *"Oh, I just imagined that"* or *"Oh, he/she isn't THAT scary"* or *"I'm not happy about how he just hurt me, but he probably won't do it again."* Does that sound like you? If so, stop ignoring your internal warning system. Red flags are there for your protection.

Day #165

Even though I intend a good outcome for every task on my To-do list each day, I remain open to the fact that I don't know what that should be for each one. I'm not God. Only he knows what's best. But what I can do is saturate each task with positive energy. That way I stay in a good place to help others. You can do this, too. Try it today.

Day #166

If you're a survivor of child abuse, your home was dangerous and your parents or caretakers couldn't be trusted. That's not what you want for your kids. Learn to discipline your kids in an empathetic, proactive way. Instead of shaming a struggling child, connect with that child's struggle. This encourages and empowers them to ask for support in situations like this. You validate their worth by inviting them to concentrate on their strengths, not their weaknesses. In the process, you'll raise children who trust you to have their best interests at heart.

Day #167

Become the person others share their wins with. Don't be the person others hide their success from for fear of judgement or ridicule. Nothing will stop the flow of your abundance faster than that kind of negative energy. It's the opposite of Love. It's Lack. Avoid it whenever you can.

Day #168

When learning how to be comfortable with your emotions, it's important to correctly identify them. Some are real (what you truly feel). Some are learned (a conditioned response from the past). Some are perceived (you sense what someone else is feeling, and you feel it, too).

Day #169

As you begin to feel better on the inside, your outside world will change. For example, you're more mindful of how you feel in different situations and how people relate to you. Suddenly, you realize for the first time in your life you don't know who you are anymore. Are you at that point? If so, congratulations! That's a very good sign.

Day #170

How can you tell you're healing? You can handle discomfort and celebrate imperfection.

Day #171

Society tells us our value is determined by material wealth and our accomplishments. That's not true. We came into this world as spirits of Divine Love, knowing we have great worth. But because of abuse or trauma, we begin to doubt our value. This is a misconception. No matter what has happened to you in the past, you're just as valuable as you were before the abuse or trauma. That's the truth.

Day #172

This journey called "Life" is full of surprises. Each twist and turn prepares you for the next step on your journey. If you put your trust in God, he will guide you exactly where you're supposed to go. You'll be in the perfect place at the perfect time. Always. God is amazing, isn't he?!

Day #173

Life is the School. Love is the Lesson. This is always my focus. The healing journey taught me that living a life of Love is the mark of all thrivers. I know it sounds simple. Sometimes, it's too simple. But Love is truly all that matters. What small step can you take today to begin living a life of Love?

Day #174

God teaches you how to listen to the promptings in your spirit by giving you signs in your everyday life. What has God been telling you lately about the next step on your healing journey? Watch for signs. They always appear to verify his quiet promptings in your spirit. Don't worry. You'll recognize them immediately when you see them.

Day #175

Get into the habit of searching for the "silver lining" in every moment of the day. It's actually been scientifically proven this way of looking at life has an astounding impact on your brain. It's no wonder it will help you overcome the challenges on the healing journey more easily.

Day #176

Are you stuck on your healing journey? There's a reason for that. Healing requires stepping out of our comfort zone, and this terrifies the subconscious. Yes, we know we're stuck and miserable. But it's familiar territory. We feel we can manage it. If we venture out and move beyond this dysfunctional safety zone, we'll no longer have complete control. Eeeek! Scary stuff. This is why you're stuck. Take a small step out of your comfort zone today and see what happens.

Day #177

Peace on the in-side. Peace on the out-side. Nature is a wonderful example of the many facets of life. Sometimes the sky is stormy, but the sun always comes out after it rains. Cultivate inner peace and watch the sun come out inside you, too.

Day #178

Do certain conversation topics make you feel threatened? Child abuse survivors have lots of triggers. If a certain subject gives you an instant feeling of fear, you need to address this. Triggers are signs you have deeper work to do on your healing journey. Triggers are friends in disguise.

Day #179

You're not your fears. You're not your challenges. You're not your doubts. Don't choose those things. Choose the "real" you instead. Choose your authentic self. There's incredible freedom in that.

Day #180

Intent is the key to manifestation. It's where you begin. Intent adds an extra boost to your goals and helps them manifest faster. What is your intention for your healing journey? Write it down and hang it in a place where you'll see it every day.

Day #181

You deserve everything GOOD in life. Yes, you do! But it all starts with a plan. Let this year be the year you manifest your healing goals. Make them your intent, and then create a plan to manifest them. You can do this. Go for it!

Day #182

An important step on the healing journey for any abuse or trauma survivor is to start talking about what happened to you. Break the silence. Ask for assistance, preferably from a therapist or coach, who can help you deal with the effects of this kind of trauma. These professionals understand what you're going through. You need that kind of support and validation right now.

Day #183

Love is a lifestyle choice, and it begins with how you treat your body. Love for ourselves, love for others, love for God, and God's love for us. This connection is all that truly matters in life. Begin to experience it today.

Day #184

My connection to the spiritual energy source in nature has become one of my most important self-care tools. If you're not there yet, don't give up. Keep trying to tap into this powerful support system offered to us by the earth and sky until it feels good. Trust me. It's worth it.

Day #185

You need support. You need that human connection. But how do you do that? You take a chance and reach out. Peer support groups, coaching, or therapy will help you reconnect with others. Who can you reach out to today?

Day #186

Reconnecting with your personal power will upset the dynamic of all your relationships. Some will be thrilled for you. Some will be horrified. Don't worry. This happens to everyone.

Day #187

Self-care begins the healing journey to the heart. It begins with you falling in love with yourself.

Day #188

Learning how to love yourself is hard in the beginning for survivors of child abuse. We learned how to disconnect from the truth about ourselves and others in order to survive. Go slow. Be patient with yourself. You'll get there.

Day #189

The most important thing survivors of emotional abandonment, abuse, and trauma want is to be seen and heard. We all crave it. Nothing means more to us than someone who truly listens to us and gets us. It validates us as human beings.

Day #190

How should you begin each day? With kindness, gratitude, and the truth of who you are.

Day #191

I'm grateful I've learned how to "hear" my body's quiet voice and to honor those requests. It's taken me years to get to this point. But it was well worth the effort. What is your body telling you today? Listen to that quiet, nagging whisper inside you. Does it need more rest, a more nutritious diet, some self-care time? Whatever it needs, honor that request today.

Day #192

Do you know what's the last hurdle to healing? It's "love." Not only do you resist allowing people to love you, but you also resist being kind and loving to yourself. Why? You believe you have no value or worth. Think about that today. Does the idea of loving yourself make you nervous?

Day #193

Continue to love yourself. Continue to love everyone you meet. Continue to love how awesome your life is becoming. Continue to love every single thing you encounter. Soon the impossible will become possible. Suddenly, you won't even have to try anymore. Love will be all you can do.

Day #194

This crazy, chaotic world needs more love. But how can you love everyone? Especially strangers? You can't. Trust and feeling safe aren't easy for trauma and abuse survivors. Fortunately, we are just the vessels Divine Love flows through. Let it flow today. That's all you have to do.

Day #195

Protecting the secret of abuse is the root of your pain. The price you pay by not acknowledging the truth of who you are is just too high.

Day #196

Every trauma survivor is triggered by the violence in our world. After years of living in fear, you know its power all too well. Don't give fear that power. Don't allow it to rule your life. Let today be the last day it terrorizes you!

Day #197

Open yourself to miracles today. After years of expecting the worst, I now expect good things in my life. Do you still expect the worst? Change that false belief today. You attract the same kind of energy you put out. Begin putting out positive energy by expecting miracles. It won't be easy at first, but stick with it. Soon it will come naturally. Then watch the miracles appear!

Day #198

The sense of urgency you feel is part of the normal "fight or flight" survival response. It's how the human brain responds to change or a threat. However, in our case, it became chronic and toxic due to the months or years of abuse and trauma we endured.

Day #199

You are worthy of self-love. Learn how to be good at this. It's one of the most important skills you'll acquire on your healing journey.

Day #200

The minute a "red flag" appears over someone's behavior, pay careful attention to it. Your internal warning system is built on discernment (noticing red flags) and setting firm boundaries with the people in your life.

Day #201

Every morning I take a few minutes to meditate on my intentions for the day. I visualize and "feel" my tasks, appointments, etc. As I do, I add the power of positive emotion to each task, intending the best outcome for each one. Have you ever done this? If not, try it. It makes a BIG difference in the quality of your day.

Day #202

You will thrive on your healing journey if you continue to be endlessly curious about how humans heal and restore. You should always be reading books and articles, watching videos, cruising YouTube, and devouring blog posts and newsletters about change, empowerment, and trauma. What are you reading this week?

Day #203

There is more than enough in this world for all of us. Be happy for others when they are blessed. Celebrate their success, as if it were your own. Why? Because when you're happy for others, you're completely open to receiving your own abundance. Thoughts of lack no longer block your path to success.

Day #204

As an abused child, you were terrified of expressing your feelings. You knew it would get you into trouble. The abuse trained you to disconnect from your emotions. But this toxic coping skill imprisons you in a constant state of numbness. How do you begin to feel again? Start with awareness. You've always been aware of your feelings. You're just in the habit of suppressing them. Stop doing that today. When you feel an emotion, stop and recognize it. Give it a name like love, fear, anxiety, pain, grief, happiness, despair, sadness, joy, etc. That's the first step.

Day #205

The more I connect with my heart the closer I feel to God. Once I realized this, I immediately felt compelled to love others. Much to my surprise, I discovered the love I send forth blesses me as much as it blesses those around me. Try it today!

Day #206

How can you tell you're healing? You're no longer controlled by triggers.

Day #207

When you've reached the point where you know who this new, healthy YOU is and you're proud of it, congratulations! This is a major milestone in your healing. Are you there today? If not, how close are you? You're probably closer than you think.

Day #208

We're all valuable human beings. Part of the healing journey is facing your fears, accepting your broken parts, and shining a light on those dark places. This is part of forgiving yourself for the things you did and said before you began your healing journey.

Day #209

No matter how busy life gets, I make sure I'm still at the top of my priority list. My self-care is what matters the most to me. How are you caring for yourself today?

Day #210

Trusting God on your healing journey isn't one big goal you finally achieve, and then you're done. Instead, just when you think you trust God 100%, he reveals a bunch of small areas in which you *should* trust him, but you don't. Yikes! What small area of trust is God revealing to you today?

Day #211

Thoughts and the words they inspire are containers of power. They're creative forms of energy. This is how you rebuild your life and grow from a survivor of abuse and trauma to an empowered thriver. You do it one positive thought at a time.

Day #212

How do you embrace the changes you need to make in order to heal? How do you find the courage to escape the tiny, safe world you've built for yourself? Reaching out for support made all the difference for me. It might be what you need, too. Consider reaching out today.

Day #213

When you begin to live your truth, there's no going back. What is your truth? It's who you are. It's why you do what you do. This knowledge supports you more than you can imagine.

Day #214

Use a "treasure map" to manifest your goals for your healing journey. To create a treasure map, gather words, pictures, and any flat items that represent your goals. Then glue or tape them in a collage on a piece of cardboard. This is your treasure map. Hang it in a place where you'll see it every day. The power of making your goals visual is amazing. It's a wonderful form of constant reinforcement!

Day #215

Trauma and abuse disconnect you from your heart and feelings. Healing from trauma teaches you to be intentional about reconnecting with others. But until you learn how to reconnect with yourself, you'll continue to struggle in your relationships with others.

Day #216

Do you need to strengthen your personal or emotional boundaries? If so, choose one to work on this month.

Day #217

When you truly value who you are, you'll have no problem setting emotional boundaries with the narcissists in your life. If taking care of yourself first and valuing who you are upsets these people, this just means they feel they have more value than you. You serve a purpose in their lives. That's all. Self-care makes it easier for you to say, *"NO"* to narcissists. Be loving, but firm with them.

Day #218

It's easy for abuse and trauma survivors to forget change is a growth process. Ups and downs are part of it. Learn to appreciate the goals you reach, as well as the bumps in the road along the way. Each one appeared to teach you an important lesson that will lead you to future success.

Day #219

Healing takes great courage. But guess what? Survivors of abuse and trauma are some of the most courageous people I know. And you're one of those courageous people. How do I know this? Because you're a survivor of abuse or trauma. It's takes great courage to survive trauma. Today, direct that courageous energy into your healing.

Day #220

Here's some good news. You can heal your body from the effects of trauma without having to relive all those painful memories. Tension is just energy. It needs to be gently felt and released. When that happens, the body is free to heal itself. It will regenerate and replace stored trauma with feelings of peace. Hallelujah!

Day #221

You have to disconnect from your body, emotions, and other people in order to survive abuse or trauma. Unfortunately, this is a coping skill that helps you survive during abuse or trauma, but does not serve you afterwards. At that point, disconnection becomes toxic and sabotages everything in your life. Ouch! Think about this today. Find one way to connect with your body, emotions, or other people and practice that today.

Day #222

What would you be doing if you felt completely accepted, loved, and adored right now? Think about it.

Day #223

To be more loving to others, develop an inner awareness of your energy when you interact with people. Do you automatically get defensive so you won't be hurt? Or do you remain calm, open, and trusting? To figure this out, don't ask your mind. Instead, focus on your body. It will let you know instantly if you're defensive or calm.

Day #224

As abused children, we learned at an early age how to be silent and invisible. If your abusers couldn't see you, they couldn't blast you with hurtful words or do painful things to you, right? It was a great survival strategy, and it worked really well. However, it's a terrible behavior pattern for an adult. Staying silent and invisible makes a mess out of your personal relationships.

Day #225

The emotional abusers in your life may be family, friends, co-workers, or your spouse. Don't allow these people to violate your emotional boundaries. Remember, your truth defines your boundaries. Your boundaries say you deserve to be treated with love and respect. No exceptions!

Day #226

Take the time today to look around you. What do you see? If you look hard enough, you'll see plenty of signs throughout your day reminding you of this fact: God loves you. Always!

Day #227

Even when you finally make the transition from survivor to thriver, you'll continue to grow and learn. Any change will still bring discomfort. But you'll no longer be terrified of the total disorder change brings. You can handle discomfort now. It's not the end of the world, because you love and trust yourself and know you'll make it through.

Day #228

If you work at it, you can truly love everyone and everything. Yes, it seems like an impossible task at first. But I've learned I can always love more, hold more love, and give more love. Try it today. You'll see!

Day #229

No matter what kind of trauma you endured, God has been there all along, working his perfect plan for your life. You're not alone, and you never have been. Pray to God about it today. He always answers!

Day #230

Speaking your truth is one of the hardest and most important steps child abuse survivors need to take on their healing journey. When you were a child, you survived the abuse by pushing it away. That's how you managed the pain. But that toxic coping skill will sabotage your adult life. You must acknowledge your truth, journal about it, and talk about it with safe people. Doing so releases the inner tension caused by decades of hiding your truth. It begins the healing process by tapping into the healing power of your authentic self.

Day #231

When you finally realize how hard you've been on yourself it's an incredibly freeing experience. But it's also frightening. You were never taught how to be good to yourself. How do you start? Begin by choosing a kind word for yourself today. Then another. And another.

Day #232

Your heart is patient. Did you know that? It's true. Your heart trusts you'll eventually find your way back to it. It has faith in you. Always.

Day #233

When something is uncomfortable (even a good change), you want to push through it quickly. That's just the normal "fight or flight" response that has become toxic in you due to chronic abuse and trauma.

Day #234

Most child abuse survivors resist the concept of self-love. They don't know what it looks like, or how it's supposed to feel. That's because no one was kind to us or showed us how to be kind to ourselves. Because we never learned these skills as children, we grew up treating ourselves in very unkind ways. How have you treated yourself in an unkind way this month? After you apologize to yourself, create a compassionate response to replace your unkind response for each of those times.

Day #235

If you were abused as a child, you had to disconnect from the truth in order to survive. Even though you were up to your eyeballs in "red flags," you had to ignore them to survive an abusive situation. Eventually, this became one of your toxic coping skills. How do you ignore red flags as an adult? Do you rationalize and talk yourself out of them?

Day #236

Even if you've made the decision to center your life around nourishing your authentic self, it will be an ongoing process. It's a challenge for everyone to accept responsibility for themselves and their wellbeing, but especially for abuse and trauma survivors like us. I won't kid you. It can be really hard sometimes. But it gets easier month after month.

Day #237

When I began my healing journey, I realized I didn't know much about parenting. I could keep my two little girls fed, clean, and safe. But I didn't know how to interact with them, listen to them, play with them, direct them, or empower them. I realized an important part of my healing would be learning how to become a good parent to myself, since mine couldn't be trusted when I was a child. Think about this today. Are you a good parent to yourself? How?

Day #238

Give yourself permission to celebrate yourself progress every day on your healing journey. You're extremely precious and valuable to all of us. Now more than ever, the world needs you and the wonderful gift you were born with. Don't hide it. Let it shine!

Day #239

One of the hardest things for me to do on my healing journey was to comfortably acknowledge my feelings. I had no idea why I felt the way I did, or how to express my emotions. Like you, chronic child abuse and trauma taught me to shut down my emotions when faced with an uncomfortable situation. I was terrified of these bottled-up emotions. They were so intense! Do you express your trapped emotions? Or do you go numb so you can't feel anything?

Day #240

We all need to "feel" loved. We all struggle with this, because we don't believe we're worthy of love. Instead, we feel rejected and abandoned. These negative feelings are from the past. But they'll remain with us forever until we learn to love ourselves first. What loving thing can you do for yourself today?

Day #241

How can you tell you're healing? You no longer feel the need to hide.

Day #242

How do you know you're finally living your truth? When you're the same person with everyone. No more people-pleasing. No more codependent behavior. No more masks to wear. There's no need for these crutches. Your heart is finally free!

Day #243

The brain is an amazing organ. But sometimes it can block your healing. That's because what helps us survive chronic abuse and trauma is not what heals us. Do you feel stuck lately? Your brain could be sabotaging you. Be gentle with yourself. Your brain just needs time to adjust to your latest healing change.

Day #244

Make a list of the things you're ready to release in your life. Pray as you let each one go. Then give it to God. Be intentional. Listen to your heart. Deep down you know what you're ready to release and walk away from. Trust that knowing.

Day #245

Trusting God is a lifelong process. Human nature is very complex in areas of trust, especially if you were an abused child. Think about your relationship with God. Where is it today? What areas of trust do you need to work on?

Day #246

Trusting God on your healing path requires action and intent. Take action by deciding which area of your life needs more faith in God. Then set your intention and work on slowly building your faith in that area every day. One tiny step at a time. That's how it happens.

Day #247

You may have found a safe place for yourself, but now you're stuck in it. Every step of the healing journey requires risk. Every step challenges you to change, to move out of your comfort zone. And that can be terrifying. What part of the healing journey scares you today? How do you plan to move through that fear to continue on the healing path?

Day #248

Say this affirmation to yourself: *I'm proud of who I am!* Place your hand over your heart to add a gentle, soothing touch to the healing energy of these words. Feel the warmth of someone who truly loves and cares about you. Practice this every day. It'll change your life.

Day #249

Your heart wants to be your personal cheerleader. However, it's up to you to take action. Tune out fear, tune into your heart, and take that next step on your healing journey!

Day #250

There are always things we feel we absolutely cannot do on the healing journey. How do you overcome this challenge? Just change your mind about it. I'm not kidding! That's all you have to do. Change your mind about something, and everything will work out to support that change. There may be a little kicking and screaming at first (lol), but that change will manifest in your life and bear fruit.

Day #251

Your negative emotions are your friends. Did you wake up feeling sad this morning? Rather than rationalize it away, embrace it. Concentrate on it. Why are you feeling sad? Sooner or later it will tell you. When it does, you can decide how to deal with it.

Day #252

Asking and intending for good things to happen is the fast track to manifestation. What are you currently struggling with on your healing path? What new, healthy coping skill are you trying to master? What is your latest goal on your healing path? Whatever it is, make it into an intention and then ask for it. It will happen.

Day #253

It takes courage to walk away from your past. But the past is nothing more than a heavy bag of rocks you've been carrying on your back for years. Ouch! It's time to lighten your load. Today, make the decision to drop your painful past and move forward on your healing journey. You don't need the past anymore.

Day #254

The healing journey requires a loving approach to your body. When you're compassionate with your body, you'll be compassionate with others. When you're gentle with your body, you'll be gentle with others.

Day #255

One of the most important things you can do is "reconnect." You had to disconnect from your body and emotions to survive the abuse or trauma. You had to cut yourself off from the people around you to be able to manage the pain of trauma. Begin reconnecting today by connecting with the soothing, peaceful energy of nature. That's a good first step.

Day #256

Did you know humans have at least 60,000 thoughts each day, and 90% of those thoughts are about separation? Wow! Trauma and abuse isolate you. 90% of your thoughts add to that separation. However, you can't heal in isolation. These thoughts will continue to make you feel disconnected until you're mindful of them and seek human connections.

Day #257

What is your personal power? It's the ability to connect with any healthy, nourishing thing that makes you feel good about yourself. The more you connect with these things, the more power you'll rediscover within yourself.

Day #258

When daily self-care becomes a top priority in your life, it transforms you into a better person, parent, spouse, and friend. Self-care makes you a kinder human being.

Day #259

An important aspect of loving yourself is learning how to be kind to all the different parts of yourself. Especially those parts you have rejected or abandoned.

Day #260

When you were an abused child, you learned how to become invisible to stay off the radar of the people who were hurting you. You learned how to creep down the stairs, quiet as a mouse. You could slip silently out of a room. You would stand in the shadows in a dark corner. You even hunched your shoulders to appear smaller. Did you do that? Look in the mirror. Is your posture straight? If not, begin standing straight today. You deserve to be seen!

Day #261

"Belittling" is a form of emotional abuse. This is someone who criticizes or makes fun of everything about you (how you look, dress, talk, your weight, your decisions, your intelligence, etc.). If there is someone in your life like this, now you know why belittling hurts so much and has caused you so much pain. It's emotional abuse. Period.

Day #262

God loves us no matter what. I often look back at those times when I felt totally alone. Now I can see I was still loved and supported. It's how I got through that trial. I just didn't realize it at the time.

Day #263

Your authentic self (the truth of who you are) can never be taken from you. This revelation feels awesome, doesn't it? It should. It's the real YOU!

Day #264

You are here to learn about Love. We're all here to learn about Love. Think about that today. Allow the truth of this fact to sink deeply into your heart and soul.

Day #265

Why should you place your hand over your heart? Because it releases the hormone Oxytocin, which is an anti-inflammatory hormone that speeds healing. Wow! Amazing, isn't it?

Day #266

Self-care is not only one of your emotional boundaries it's also a win/win for everyone. How? Self-care is how you model for others the loving way in which you'd like them to take care of themselves.

Day #267

Make a list of all your good qualities. Review this list every day until the revelation of your wonderfulness sinks deeply into your soul. That's when you become your own cheerleader. Yay!

Day #268

Mindfulness is an excellent way to connect with your inner self. Checking in with your heart throughout the day is another successful inner connection practice. Which works best for you? Make sure you practice it every day.

Day #269

Today, make this vital aspect of your truth into an affirmation: *There's nothing wrong with me now, and there never has been.*

Day #270

One of the first things I teach my clients is how to be kind to themselves. I help them see not only are they worthy of self-love but this is also an important part of their healing journey. How do you work self-love into your life every day?

Day #271

When you were an abused child, you had to disconnect from your internal warning system to survive. Now that you're an adult, you need to reactivate it. "Red flags" are there for your protection. Yes, it's important to learn how to love others. But that doesn't mean everyone you meet is safe and worthy of your trust.

Day #272

Even when I was a little girl I knew I was a loving person. That's my authentic self. But, like all abuse survivors, I had to disconnect from that truth in order to survive and cope with my abusive reality. Today, my life is centered around nourishing my authentic self. Even when you were a little kid you knew deep down who you were. Who was that person? When you remember, center your life around nourishing whoever that was. It's your authentic self.

Day #273

Like most survivors of child abuse, I had no role models when I was growing up. My house was dangerous, and the adults couldn't be trusted. An important part of your healing journey is learning how to be a better parent to yourself. Begin by listing all the areas in which you weren't supported as a child. These areas are important stages of development that child abuse survivors missed. Start there.

Day #274

You were born with a wonderful gift. But let me warn you. Your special gift is much larger and more awesome than you could ever imagine. Because of that, your mind will be flooded with doubts when you discover it. Don't worry. Just stop focusing on your mind. Instead, pay attention to your heart. When you can hear your heart singing, you'll know you're on the right track.

Day #275

What's your passion in life? What's the one thing you feel you must do? It's the thing you feel you were born to do. As you grow and change, your passion will change, and that's normal. If you're on a mission to seek your truth, you'll stay on the right track. You'll never go wrong when you follow your heart. Your passion will change as you do, but every step of the way will be a joy.

Day #276

Look at the trees. If they can produce new growth each spring, so can you. Have faith! God knows you will succeed at any new opportunity he brings your way. That's why he's suggesting it.

Day #277

Survivors of trauma and abuse are much needed by their local communities. Why? Because the healing journey awakens within you a deep sense of love, compassion, and empathy. You're no longer afraid to feel those emotions for yourself or others. The world needs more people like you with big, loving hearts and the courage to extend compassion to those who need a helping hand. You're an incredibly special person!

Day #278

The emotionally abusive people in your adult life give you plenty of challenging opportunities to practice setting emotional boundaries, speaking your truth, and asking for what you need. They may not be in your life forever. But they always appear at the right time. One day you'll see them as a blessing. They help us eliminate the triggers of abuse or trauma from the past. They give us great practice!

Day #279

How can you tell you're healing? You finally feel connected to every part of yourself, to other people, to nature, to God, and to all that is.

Day #280

Too often we become our own worst critics. Take the time today to be aware of that. Start by choosing a loving, forgiving, daily affirmation for yourself. This is a good one: *As I lovingly forgive myself for (fill in the blank), I choose to love and accept myself for who I am.*

Day #281

Trusting yourself on your healing journey doesn't happen all at once. It goes through stages. This is because your abusive childhood was shaped by distrust, trauma, and betrayal. So we have to teach ourselves how to trust. It takes a while. Be patient with yourself. It will happen.

Day #282

What are you willing to consider as a new possibility today? Remain open to that possibility and then turn it over to God. As soon as you do, something will shift. I love how that happens!

Day #283

Are you stuck on your healing journey? Reach out for support. Surround yourself with a support system of likeminded peers, people who truly get you and know how it feels to be stuck. These are the ones who are willing to do whatever it takes to break free and change. You can do that, too. Let them help you.

Day #284

Be proud of who you are. Let me say this again, because I can't stress it enough: BE PROUD OF WHO YOU ARE! This is so powerful. I say this to myself, my kids, and my coaching clients all the time. Do you say this to yourself every day? If not, begin today. It's a vital step on your healing journey.

Day #285

Put self-care at the top of your list today. How? One day you can reach out for support. The next day do something good for your body. The next day read an inspiring book. And so on. Take action every single day to prove to yourself you're serious about your healing.

Day #286

Make your negative emotions your friends. Rather than ignore a negative emotion like you usually do, concentrate on it. Watch it. Feel it. What does it feel like? Listen to it. What is it telling you? When you know its message, you can deal with it.

Day #287

Now that you've come this far on your healing journey, you've probably had a chance to review your progress. Don't focus on what you haven't accomplished. That's not important. The only thing that matters is what you have accomplished. Celebrate your accomplishments all day long today!

Day #288

Most abuse and trauma survivors invest more emotional energy in what they struggle with (anger, grief, pain, anxiety, etc.) than they do in a happy vision of a healed life. Today, make the decision to feed your happy vision rather than your struggles. When you do, you'll be eliminating a major roadblock to your healing. Good riddance, right?!

Day #289

An important step on the healing journey is acknowledging the trauma from the past stored in your body. Do you know how to release it in a healthy way? First, acknowledge its presence. Watch it as you feel it. Then allow it to pass through your body and out. Be compassionate and patient with yourself and your body during this process. You'll feel so free afterwards. It's an awesome experience!

Day #290

When nothing seems to work, do this. Walk outside in the yard for a moment. What do you see? Trees, leaves, grass, soil, sun, clouds, sky. No matter your spiritual path, you know the energy of the earth is spiritual. The cleansing, healing energy of nature grounds and supports us. Because we live on the earth, we are connected to it in a very special, spiritual way. Take advantage of that when nothing is working out the way you planned.

Day #291

You have power. Lots of it! To connect with your personal power, you must change the false belief that you're powerless.

Day #292

Support groups can be a powerful healing tool. You learn how others are struggling and healing, and how to apply that to your own life. Have you been thinking about joining a peer support group or a new group? Take a chance and do it today. You'll be glad you did.

Day #293

To stop neglecting yourself, create a self-care regime. Begin by doing something nurturing and kind for yourself. Eat lunch in the park, take a relaxing bath, call a good friend, read a new book, work on a favorite craft, or go window shopping. Today, do what feels good to YOU!!

Day #294

Loving yourself is the thing most abuse and trauma survivors resist the most. Why? Because it's a two-fold problem for us. First, we've developed the false belief that we are unlovable. Second, since we don't know how to love ourselves, we make others responsible for loving us. But that never works, because we don't know how to accept their love. Yikes! That's our dilemma. The good news is this: we can change. Are you ready?

Day #295

Remember how it used to be? When you were an abused child, you learned the advantages of silence. In fact, you were so quiet, you hoped you would disappear. Remember that? If those memories make you anxious or depressed, release that energy by acknowledging it, feeling it, watching it, and then allowing it to pass through your body and out. Free it. There is great healing in releasing old, toxic energy in this way.

Day #296

Cut all emotional abusers out of your life. You don't need them. If some are family members, limit your time with them.

Day #297

God is always sending us this reminder: we are loved! Love is all around us. Even when we backtrack, stall out, or get stuck, love is there. Especially during those times when we feel lost or things aren't working out like we planned. God loves you no matter what. Don't forget that!

Day #298

Today, list all the positive things that are true about you. This list is your truth. No matter what happened to you or who hurt you, your truth will always be true. Meditate on this list every morning. Allow it to sink into your heart and soul.

Day #299

I'm not my pain. You're not your pain. We're not the things that happened to us when we were abused or traumatized. It's not your fault, not your shame, not your secret, and certainly not your burden to carry.

Day #300

Why should you place your hand over your heart? Because it releases the hormone Oxytocin, which reduces stress and anxiety by increasing trust and empathy.

Day #301

Self-care is not selfish. Far from it. A good self-care regime is your responsibility to yourself and to those you love. It's how you demonstrate your value and worth. The people who love you will value you more when you begin to value yourself. Think about that today.

Day #302

One day it will be impossible for you to say anything abusive to yourself. You'll simply love yourself too much. And that's the way it should be.

Day #303

You cannot love another until you learn how to love yourself. The same is true of the connection you crave. You can't connect with another until you learn how to connect with yourself (your heart).

Day #304

If you don't see the value in healing for yourself, do it for your kids, spouse, or family. That's a good place to start.

Day #305

Self-love is a necessity, not a luxury. You are more than worthy of abundant self-love every day. Never forget that. Self-love is a vital part of the healing journey. You can't heal without it.

Day #306

There's no way around it. The entire healing process takes time. You can't fast forward from the beginning to the middle to the end without doing all the necessary work in-between those major stages. That's the only way to heal. Each tiny, daily step is vital for healing from abuse or trauma.

Day #307

If you truly knew who you are, what would your day look like, and what would you be doing right now? Deep down you know who you are. You always have. Why not begin living that knowing today?

Day #308

Marriage can be rough if you're a survivor of child abuse. You and your spouse may have no idea how to be kind, understanding, and gentle with each other. Instead, the way you speak may be more like pouring salt on each other's wounds. Ouch! The turning point will come when you learn how to be friends. To do this, become accountable for all the ways you respond to each other. Soon you'll no longer expect the worst from every discussion.

Day #309

Did you know you were born with a wonderful gift? It's true! But what if you haven't discovered your special gift? Not a problem. Keep walking down this path called Life. Keep praying for revelation. Keep moving forward on your healing journey. Soon you'll be very clear about the wonderful gift you've been given.

Day #310

Apply "hope" to your healing journey. Make it your passion. Keep pushing forward, confident the next book, support group, speaker, video, or webinar will be the key to a big breakthrough. Every single breakthrough on your healing journey will happen in this way.

Day #311

Are you growing, or have you plateaued out? Has God been encouraging you to take the next step on your path? Are you moving forward into this new opportunity? Or have you been ignoring God's voice because stepping into unfamiliar territory is scary?

Day #312

The desire to reach out and help others heal is an excellent sign. It means you're passed the halfway mark on your healing journey. Is that how you feel? If so, what is the desire of your heart when it comes to helping others? Whatever it might be, go for it. You can do this!

Day #313

Believe it or not, the emotionally abusive people in your adult life are a gift and a blessing. They come into your life for a certain amount of time to show you what you need to heal in your life. Think about it. What lessons have the abusers in your life taught you? When you finally began to heal those areas vulnerable to them, it was such a blessing to you, wasn't it?

Day #314

How can you tell you're healing? You no longer feel so alone. You've reached out, and you know you're not the only survivor of child abuse or trauma. You've got proof you're not alone anymore. You have support to validate you on this journey.

Day #315

How do you move forward on the healing journey? First, you embrace your imperfections. Next, you release what no longer serves you. Are you ready to do this?

Day #316

Do you feel stuck today? Do you feel like you've plateaued out? Relax. That's normal. It will pass if you don't get frustrated and give up on yourself. Don't allow impatience to sabotage your progress. Keep moving forward. Keep gathering information on healing. Keep reaching out for support when you need it. This is the only way to heal.

Day #317

What do you do when your mind says you can't do something? Rather than argue with it, I say: *"Okay, I'm just going to consider the possibility that I can do this. I'm not actually stepping out into the unknown and doing anything. I'm just considering the possibility."* That soothes the fearful part of my mind.

Day #318

Trusting God is a lifelong process. It's like reading a book with 10,000 pages in it, and each page is a different area of trust. What a fun adventure, right? I think so!

Day #319

Are you suddenly feeling angry for no reason? Your negative feelings are your friends. Rather than ignore this sudden feeling of anger, concentrate on it. Sooner or later it will tell you the reason it appeared. Then you can decide what kind of action to take.

Day #320

There's so much to be grateful for when you make the decision to live only in the present moment. The hidden joys in each day no longer pass you by.

Day #321

Make yourself a top priority. Do this every day. It's the only way to create the necessary internal shift from living in fear to living in hope.

Day #322

Don't allow the chaos of life and the challenges on your healing journey to prevent you from taking care of yourself first. Be kind and compassionate to yourself. Slow down when you feel overwhelmed. Scale back your To-Do list to a manageable number. Self-care is the key to success on the healing journey.

Day #323

The path to self-trust is an inward journey. It's a skill you learn through experience. To begin, find a quiet moment and place your hand on your heart. Ask your heart what it thinks about each choice you need to make throughout this day.

Day #324

Today, create a list of everything you're tired of struggling with: the pain, the grief, the sadness, the hopelessness, the fear (all your fears), the anger, the frustration, the anxiety, etc. Also include everything you want to release. This list is what's blocking your healing. It's the burden of your past. Make today the day you drop your past and walk away from it forever.

Day #325

Your body absorbs more information than you're consciously ready to receive. You might not remember everything that happened to you when you were abused or traumatized, but your body remembers all of it. Your body is a storehouse for all the trauma and stress you've ever experienced. Learn how to express your feelings safely and connect with your mind/body/spirit. It's an important part of your healing journey.

Day #326

God, Love, Father Sky, Universe, Spirit, Angels, Mother Nature, etc. It doesn't matter what you call your Higher Power. It's your safety net. Use it when the going gets tough on your healing journey. It's there for you. Always.

Day #327

You must love and accept yourself first before others will love and accept you. Think about it. How would your world change if you felt completely loved and accepted? See that vision in your mind. Live that life and be that person. Do it today. Begin by taking small steps. But keep moving forward. That's how self-acceptance sinks into your soul and stays there.

Day #328

Many adult survivors of child abuse continue to neglect themselves in the same way they were neglected. Do you neglect your needs by not giving yourself the love, compassion, empathy, and self-care your body and mind are asking for? Why do you do that?

Day #329

No matter what type of abuse you survived, all abuse survivors are emotionally neglected. Emotional neglect (abandonment) is the most damaging kind of abuse. It creates a sense of unworthiness in survivors. Stop neglecting yourself today. To do that, place your hand over your heart, look in the mirror, and say this simple affirmation: *I love you.* Keep saying this to your mirror image until you believe it.

Day #330

The issue of love is a struggle for all abuse survivors. You can feel terribly broken when you realize you don't know how to love yourself. But don't beat yourself up about it. Knowing this is a blessing. You've just taken your first step toward self-love. Congratulations!

Day #331

Practice mindfulness every day. Place your hand on your heart, take a few deep mindful breaths, and say to yourself: *"I am here now. I am safe now. Everything is okay right now in this moment. I am loved. I am here for me. I am enough. God supports me every step of the way."*

Day #332

Your body has retained much of the stress from your abusive or traumatized past. That trauma is trapped and will eventually manifest as physical pain and/or disease. Your body knows how to release blocked trauma and restore itself to a calm, natural state. Learn how to work with your body to heal itself. Make a trauma releasing technique like tapping, TRE, mindfulness, meditation, etc., a daily practice.

Day #333

"Interrupting" is a form of emotional abuse. This is someone who constantly interrupts everything you say by changing the subject. Is there someone like this in your adult life right now? If so, now you know why you feel so crummy when this happens. It's classic abuse.

Day #334

You are a valuable spirit of the Divine. You are worthy. You deserve to be seen AND heard. Today is a good day to take that chance. Go for it!

Day #335

Remember, the truth is always true. You have the power to decide what's true for you and what isn't. Here are some things that will always be true: you're a good person, you're loveable, you're enough, you're valuable, you're a blessing, you're a miracle. Embrace your truth today.

Day #336

This is a great affirmation for abuse and trauma survivors: ***I'm blessed to feel free. I'm free to be me.*** It still brings tears of joy and gratitude to my eyes. How about you? Say this affirmation to yourself all day today. It's your truth!

Day #337

Have you ever been mad at God? Have you ever felt like he abandoned you? Have you ever wondered why he allowed you to suffer abuse or trauma for all those years? Actually, the bad stuff has nothing to do with God. He never abandoned you. How do I know? He led you to this book!

Day #338

My wish today is for you to know you're incredibly valuable. It's true. Allow this truth to sink deeply into your soul. Remind yourself of this truth and put it into action with careful, compassionate self-care today.

Day #339

When you talk to the people you love, you're kind, compassionate, gentle, empathetic, and loving. Is this the way you talk to yourself? It should be. Pay attention to that today. If you're incredibly hard on yourself and constantly beat yourself up for not being perfect, stop doing that. This is a good way to add some self-love to your day.

Day #340

In your pain and confusion, have you been trying to replace the inner connection you crave (connecting with your heart) for something external, like lovers, activity, food, relationships, or material possessions? If so, list those today and review how dissatisfying they ultimately were.

Day #341

When you reconnect with your truth (all the good stuff that's true about you), you're able to love and respect every person on the planet. When you respect yourself, you're able to respect and honor others for who they are and what they've been through. When you learn to love yourself, you're able to truly love others.

Day #342

We live in a hurting world that desperately needs more love and compassion. We can do our part every day. We can choose to love. How are you manifesting love and compassion in your life today?

Day #343

Big changes takes months or years. But that's the beauty of living in the moment. Be good to yourself. Practice mindfulness on every step of your healing journey. Celebrate each healing stage: the beginning, the middle, the end. It's worth it, and so are you!

Day #344

Filling yourself up with the good stuff is important. If you're like me, you're a giving person. It's easier for you to help others than yourself. Of course, that doesn't work. If we don't give ourselves all the good things that nourish our body, spirit, and soul, we can't help anyone else. How are you filling yourself up today?

Day #345

If you're married and struggling with how to communicate to your partner about your healing journey, work on strengthening your relationship as friends. Don't argue or bicker. Instead, practice being kind, gentle, and compassionate with each other. If you seek peace in your relationship, you will find it. It begins by building a good, solid friendship.

Day #346

Changing old toxic beliefs from your childhood is an ongoing, intentional process. Yes, bad things happened to you in the past. But that doesn't mean you deserve bad things today. Survivors of abuse and trauma must choose what they believe, moment by moment, day after day, year after year. Choose wisely. Choose nourishing beliefs that bless you.

Day #347

When a child is abused by someone that child loves and depends on, the child will create a story about how the abuse is really the child's fault. Not the fault of the parent or guardian. It's the only way to survive the abuse. That story gave you hope. It promised if you could just be better and do better the abuse would stop. That story never worked, but it trained you to hope. Let hope drive you to do whatever you can to heal yourself. This time it will work. Why? Because this time you're in charge!

Day #348

Cultivate the habit of listening closely to your heart. The answer you receive will always be the right one for you. Your heart never lies.

Day #349

I've written this on a sticky note and attached it to a wall I see often: **When I'm Distracted, I'm Disconnected**. If distraction is one of your toxic coping skills, try this. It's a visual reminder that works.

Day #350

Your traumatized subconscious tries to write a happy ending to your story. It does that by attracting emotionally abusive people into your adult life. It wants them to love, understand, and value you. It wants them to finally "get" you. Of course, they can't. Most emotional abusers have no desire to change. If you've ever wondered why you attract abusive people like this, now you know.

Day #351

As you progress along your healing journey, do you realize you're also helping others? You are. Just by being a loving, kind, grounded person, you're becoming an example of how to live a meaningful, wholehearted life.

Day #352

How do you focus your intent? Beginning each day grounded with focused intent is a conscious act that puts you in charge of yourself and your day. If you don't begin each day like this, your subconscious takes over. Then you're operating on autopilot, which means you no longer control your destiny. Yikes!

Day #353

Even though I'd been on my healing journey for 8 years and had made great progress, my marriage was in shambles. I hadn't realized how the trauma from my abusive childhood was sabotaging my marriage. We fought constantly about almost everything. I had healed a lot, but I was still defensive, disconnected, and afraid. Finally, we got professional help and learned how to communicate in a healthy way. Now my marriage is rock solid, and we've become best friends. If your marriage is being sabotaged by the trauma or abuse you survived, what kind of help can you reach out for today to improve your communication skills with your spouse?

Day #354

Lately, I've been trusting God in a new area of my life. I'm practicing trust in my spiritual growth like never before. Whew! Getting serious about the spiritual path is both humbling and powerful. Trusting anyone after trauma is a growth process that requires action and intent. Are you doing the same? If so, what is your intent and the corresponding action? Stick with it!

Day #355

Who would you be without the pain from your past? Think about that today. Don't allow the pain from your past to sabotage your healing.

Day #356

Today, I'm grateful. I'm grateful for my coaching clients, Facebook followers, email list subscribers, blog readers, family, friends, home, cats, health, strong body, compassionate heart, love for people, passion to live life to the fullest, God, nature, trees, waterfalls, and the abundant universe. What are you grateful for today?

Day #357

How do you walk the healing journey? One self-loving day at a time. No mysterious rescuer is coming to save you. But there's no need. You can rescue yourself. Just listen to and follow the wisdom of your heart. It knows exactly what you need to heal yourself.

Day #358

What have you given to yourself today? The gift that keeps on giving is love and compassion. This is the gift we're free to give others every day of the year. That's also the gift you should give yourself, especially when the going gets rough on your healing journey.

Day #359

How do you deal with your negative emotions? Do you avoid them, or do you appreciate the insight they provide?

Day #360

Many child abuse survivors end up in one abusive relationship after another. If that has been happening to you, you may not realize you have power. You can speak up for yourself, set healthy boundaries, and protect yourself from abusers. Don't suffer in silence like you did when you were a child. You don't have to do that anymore.

Day #361

Like most abuse and trauma survivors, I didn't get the normal amount of playtime when I was a kid. Making time for play is extremely important for us as adults. When you give your mind a break from work, your body is refreshed in healthy ways. Best of all, solutions to challenges appear out of nowhere because you changed your focus. Make scheduling time for fun a top priority today. Your body and brain will thank you!

Day #362

Today, I want to talk about self-violence. If you don't express your emotional pain you're using it against yourself and others. Unexpressed pain makes you isolate, disconnect, and suffer. The antidote? Reach out for support. You're not alone. Telling others about your pain actually relieves the pain. You have the power to stop the cycle of pain in your life. Do it today.

Day #363

When you focus on the NOW, the past loses its grip on you. However, making this adjustment isn't easy for abuse and trauma survivors. Wellness begins in the present moment with awareness, acceptance, and kindness to yourself. Use this affirmation to make the transition to the NOW easier for you: *I accept myself just the way I am, right here, right now.*

Day #364

Many of your inner struggles occur because you don't believe you have worth. What would you do differently if you knew you were enough?

Day #365

You may have begun your healing journey for your kids or spouse, but healing is something you need to do for yourself. It's how you become an empowered parent, spouse, family member, and friend, one who practices self-care, self-love, self-compassion, and self-acceptance every day. It's the only way you'll be able to create the healthy, nourishing life you've always wanted. It's the path to true freedom.

About The Author

Svava Brooks is an Abuse Survivor Coach and an international speaker on the topic of child sexual abuse.

A survivor of child sexual abuse, Svava is a certified Crisis Intervention Specialist, a certified trainer for *Darkness to Light Stewards of Children*, a certified Parent Educator, a *BellaNet Teen* support group facilitator, and a certified facilitator for the *Advance!* program by *Connections*.

She lives with her family in Oregon.

Are you an abuse or trauma survivor ready to heal? If so, I can help. Just call 619-889-6366 or send me an email (svava@educate4change.com) to reserve a one-hour coaching session with me. My calendar is filling up fast, so don't wait. Let me help you heal your life. Reserve your spot NOW!

Are you on my email list? If you'd like to receive my empowering monthly newsletter and an email with a link to my weekly blog post, go to: http://www.educate4change.com/

Svava Brooks
Abuse Survivor Coach, Facilitator, and Speaker
Portland, Oregon
619-889-6366
email: svava@educate4change.com
Website and Blog: http://www.educate4change.com
Facebook: https://www.facebook.com/educate4change
Twitter: http://www.twitter.com/svavas
LinkedIn: http://www.linkedin.com/in/svavabrooks